The Ultimate Fasting Diet

Simple Intermittent Fasting Strategies to Boost Weight Loss, Control Hunger, Fight Disease, and Slow Down Aging

D1525348

Connor Thompson

Table of Contents

Review Request

Related Books

Introduction

Congratulations and thank you for downloading this eBook.

The following chapters will discuss everything that you need to know to get started and find success with intermittent fasting. There are a lot of diet plans on the market, however, many of these will not be effective. With intermittent fasting, you will be able to stick with this diet for a long time. There are a few options, so you can go with the method that ultimately works best for you.

In this guidebook, we are going to talk about intermittent fasting and how it can work for you. We will look at the basics of the fasting method including what it is, why so many people enjoy it, and more. We will also look at easy, delicious recipes that you can use on fasting days and non-fasting days. With this guidebook, you will understand exactly what you need to do to lose weight.

Other diet plans may be difficult to follow but going on an intermittent fast can be easy. Make sure that you read through this guidebook so you can start seeing great results with little effort.

There are plenty of books on this subject on the market; thanks again for choosing this one! It's my wish to provide you with the tools you need to make your dieting goals a success.

Chapter 1: Why Most Diets Don't Work

Most people have been on a diet at some point in their life for a variety of reasons. Maybe they wanted to lose a few pounds before going on a trip or vacation; maybe they tried to lose weight to feel better about themselves but got tired, bored, and gave up on the diet; or, maybe they just wanted to look their best for their high school reunion. No matter what the reason, it's likely that the diet only worked for a short period of time. Many diet plans are too hard to stick with long term, and when a diet is too hard to follow, the tendency is to give up and revert to old eating habits. Unsurprisingly, along with old eating habits, old weight is regained as well.

These diet plans (sometimes called yo-yo diets) are hard on the body. You want to lose weight and be healthy, however, most diet plans focus only on short-term results. More importantly, these diet plans often don't have an outline for how you can maintain the diet for the long term or they are too strict for the dieter to stick with for longer than a few months.

There are many different types of diet plans for you to follow such as the Paleo Diet, the Low-Carb Diet, the Ketogenic diet, the vegetarian diet, and more. You can go on a diet plan that is going to restrict you from eating any fat and will ask you to focus on eating mostly fruits, vegetables, and a lot of carbs. Likewise, there are diet plans that will give you opposite advice and will tell you to dramatically reduce your carbs, and to instead focus on healthy fats and moderate amounts of protein. There are even diets on the market that have dieters go on a juice fast, cabbage soup diet, and other recommendations that are difficult to sustain.

While these diets can provide you with some short-term results, they are not good options if you are seeking long term results as they leave you hungry, possibly harm your body, and can even fuel negative thoughts about your self-image if you are unable to stick with the diet's unrealistic expectations. Along with these many diets, there is also a lot of conflicting advice that exists online. Think about how many times you have heard that fat is bad, and that carbs are good. However, the Ketogenic diet (which has become very popular) says the exact opposite: avoid carbs and eat more fat; this can be confusing for those who are looking to lose weight.

So, why do these diet plans ultimately fail? The main reason is that they are too strict or are too hard to follow; they are not designed for the typical person and how their busy schedule. They may have some good advice but being able to stick with them for a long period of time is quite difficult for most people. It can really hurt one's self-confidence when the diet is too demanding, and it's eventually abandoned. When it comes to weight loss, the goal should be changing your lifestyle rather than just changing the food that you consume. If you are someone who loves pasta, do you think you will be able to go on a low carb diet long term? If you are someone who loves a good steak or hamburger, do you think you will be able to stick to a vegetarian diet? Probably not.

Despite what other diet plans tell you, there is nothing wrong with eating these foods if you do so in moderation. Diets like the Ketogenic and Low-Carb diets spend too much time telling you what you are

NOT allowed to eat so it becomes tedious to follow the strict guidelines every day. Of course, you want to follow the rules that come with your chosen diet. However, when you are told that you can't have something that you crave, no matter how hard you try, it's going to be that much more tempting to give in later.

This is why many people love intermittent fasting. While there are some recommendations in regard to which foods you should eat while on the intermittent fast, none of them are set in stone. You can still enjoy the foods you love as long as they are nutritious and if you eat them during the non-fasting phase of the diet. This makes it much easier for you to have the will power to stay on course during times of craving. If you can limit yourself to eating these foods during the non-fasting phase, you will see positive results in your weight loss.

The intermittent fast is about setting realistic, achievable goals that don't require superhuman willpower. This is a diet that you can get on and stay on because you can have variety in the things you eat so that it isn't a struggle every day. The hardest part of this diet is the first few days. While beginning the fasting phase, it's likely that you will experience hunger pains as your body isn't getting the same calorie intake that it's used to. However, with persistence, your body will adapt to these changes and the discomfort will pass. After you get over this hump, you will be well on your way to seeing excellent results!

With the help of the intermittent fasting diet, you will be able to break the cycle of dieting and relapse. With this diet, you will have the tools you need to get the results you are looking for. You will lose weight, have more energy throughout your day, and start to *feel* healthy again.

Chapter 2: The Science Behind Intermittent Fasting

The intermittent fasting diet is one of the best diet plans that you can adopt and it has a lot of great options to choose from. For example, you can choose to fast every day and limit the window of time that you allow yourself to eat during the day. Another option might be to fast for an entire day, or to choose specific days that you restrict your calories. Having these options makes it easier to adapt to your lifestyle because you have the flexibility to find the option that works best for you.

There are many types of fasts that you can choose from. Some people will choose to go with the 16/8 fast, which is one of the most common. This involves fasting for 16 hours of the day while being allowed to eat for the other 8 hours. Similarly, some people will allow themselves 10 hours to eat while others will allow for only 4 hours. There is some flexibility here that can suit your needs, so it's best to adjust the times you set aside to eat and to fast that best fit your life.

There are other options that you can go with as well, such as the 5:2 diet. This involves choosing 2 days a week where you can only eat up to 500 or 600 calories the whole day.

Another option is the warrior diet where you will fast all day and then feast on the last meal of the day. Some people will choose to fast for 24 hours between meals (such as going from supper one night to supper the next day).

These are just a few of the ways to do intermittent fasting and you can choose the one that works the best for your goals and needs.

The Benefits of the Intermittent Fast

There are many benefits when it comes to intermittent fasting. Some of the best reasons to choose an intermittent fast include:

- *Weight loss*: The main reason that a lot of people choose to go on an intermittent fast is to lose weight. This diet is great not only for losing weight, but also good at burning body fat as well.

- *Fights off cancer*: There are several studies done that show how the intermittent fast can help to fight off cancer or at least prevent it from occurring in the future. [Source 1][Source 2]

- *Boost your energy*: The intermittent fast can help you gain more energy than the typical American diet. Fat is a more efficient fuel source than carbs. This allows your body to provide you with more energy, so you can make it through the day.

- *Fights off heart disease*: Intermittent fasting can help to fight heart disease as well. As your body loses weight and burns fat, your blood pressure and cholesterol levels will decrease. This make things easier on your heart. [Source 1][Source 2]

- *Helps with diabetes*: Fasting helps you to burn through fat, rather than carbs. This can keep insulin levels low and helps to treat or prevent diabetes. There are many people who decide to go on an intermittent fast and combine it with a low-carb diet to help fight off diabetes. [Source 1][Source 2]

- *Keeps away Alzheimer's*: Intermittent fasting has been linked to preventing serious brain diseases, such as Parkinson's and Alzheimer's. This is good news for anyone worried about these diseases or anyone suffering from them already. [Source 1][Source 2]

- *Adds years to your life*: There have not been too many human studies on this yet, but many folks will argue that intermittent fasting helps you to live longer. If you are looking for a simple way to look and feel younger, then the intermittent fast may *be the right option for you.* [Source 1][Source 2]`

Facts About Intermittent Fasting

Although intermittent fasting provides many benefits, it does face some criticism. For instance, some people believe fasting to be unsafe because it deprives you of calories, makes you too hungry, or makes it harder to lose weight because your body goes into starvation mode. However, these are all myths as people have been fasting for centuries all over the world to stay healthy. As with any diet, you should consult with your doctor about your dieting plans and ensure that it's appropriate for you.

It Does NOT Include Binge Eating

Many critics claim that after a fast, dieters will indulge in overeating to try and regain "lost" calories. This is not true for most people. The goal of fasting is to learn how to control your eating habits so that you consume fewer calories and lose weight. While you may binge eat when hungry on other diets, with intermittent fasting, the goal is to fast and use self-control to remain disciplined. Remember, you can adjust the way you fast to cater to your needs. If you worry that you might struggle with this, fast for less time at the beginning and gradually increase it as you get more comfortable.

Starvation

The point of this diet is to train your brain to learn what your body actually needs. When fasting, you're not starving yourself – you are teaching your body that you can go without food for periods of time. Additionally, by gaining control over your eating habits you can prevent stress-eating, a common coping mechanism. When you have practiced intermittent fasting for a while, you will have a healthier approach to food and will be more likely to eat as a way to nourish your body rather than as a way to deal with your emotions.

Hard to Follow

In some cases, people worry that this diet will be hard to follow. This can be true during the first couple of days because you are working on changing the way that your body thinks about food. It (your body) will tell you to go get something sweet or to eat more to satisfy your cravings. However, once you become accustomed to the diet, it becomes easier because you will have control over your eating habits.

You Will Always be Hungry

There are going to be times when you will feel hungry when you first get started. Keep in mind that you just need to stick with it for a couple of weeks. Once that first week is done, it will be much easier. Eventually, you will have trained yourself to respond to hunger when it's time to eat, instead of as a reaction to cravings and hunger pains.

Intermittent fasting is not something that is impossible to follow and there are some basic principles to help guide you. For example, instead of trying to change everything about your diet from quantity to food selection, this diet instead focuses on changing *when* you eat while controlling your total calories.

Chapter 3: All About the Food

Eating on the intermittent fast does not have to be a challenge. In fact, other than making sure that you remain within your allotted calories, you can technically eat whatever you want and still see great results. With that said, as with most diets, you can't expect to see the same results when you are eating unhealthy foods like cookies, hotdogs, and other processed foods compared to other healthier options like fruits and vegetables.

Some people decide to incorporate other healthy diets with the intermittent fasting. If you are going to do this, it's recommended that you go with something like the ketogenic diet which is a high-fat, moderate protein, and low-carb diet will ensure that you are able to get good results because it will keep your body burning all that extra fat.

That said, it's important to realize that you do not need to go on a specific diet or follow a specific plan to see good results when it comes to the intermittent fasting diet. As long as you are able to stick with foods that are healthy and won't take up too many calories, you are going to see improved results for your body and health.

There are a few things that you need keep in mind when it comes to working with intermittent fasting. These are not hard-set rules that you must follow all the time, but they will allow you to eat the healthy foods that are necessary to ensure that you get the best results.

First, you need to make sure that you are eating plenty of quality produce. Fruits and vegetables will have great nutrients that your body needs and are great at curbing hunger without loading up on calories. You can eat plenty of these (apples, bananas, oranges, broccoli, tomatoes, etc.) even on those fasting days; just be sure to choose fresh ingredients as well as a variety of different fruits and veggies to make sure that you get the nutrients you need. If you're having a hard time coping with hunger, this is where you should turn to curb it.

Next, you need to make sure that you are consuming adequate amounts of protein while on your diet. This does not have to be a ton but adding in a little bit with each meal will keep your muscles strong, ensuring that you will keep yourself from feeling too hungry in the process. You should go for about 20 grams or more a day for women and 25 grams or more a day for men. There are a lot of great sources that you can use to help you get protein in your diet such as chicken, pork, ground beef, turkey, and fish.

Healthy fats are also allowed, you just have to be careful because there are major differences in the types of fats that you are able to eat. Saturated fats, like those found in most fast and processed foods, are not allowed on the intermittent fast. However, healthy fats such as fish and/or beef, or options like olive oil, will ensure that you are giving the body the fuel that it needs.

Some sources of dairy are fine as well such as milk, yogurt, cheese, and sour cream as they will ensure that your body is able to get the calcium that it needs to keep your muscles strong. These dairy sources can also be nice, low-fat sources of food that work well for snacks; however, you should be careful with dairy mixed with other types of food. Items to watch out for are yogurt with fruits or chocolate, strawberry milk, chocolate milk, etc. This is because many of these foods have added sugar, which takes away from their potential nutritional value.

Next, you need to watch the kinds of carbs that you are eating. If you are going on a diet plan like the ketogenic diet, then you will have to follow specific guidelines when it comes to the carbs that you can eat. However, if you are just going on an intermittent fast, you are fine with eating some carbs as long as you do not go crazy. Most women should stay under 150 carbs a day and men under 200 carbs a day. It's important to know the difference between the different carbs that you can consume.

First, you want to watch out for any processed carbs, white bread, and grains including baked goods, candies, processed foods, most fast foods. When these get into the body, they are treated the same as sugar, and this can cause a lot of trouble to your body as too many sugars and bad carbs could result in higher insulin levels which can lead to diabetes.

On the other hand, you can also work with whole grains because they are much healthier for you. This is primarily because they take longer to digest inside the body, which means that they will keep you fuller for longer. Grains are an important source of fiber, Vitamin B, thiamin, riboflavin, niacin, folate, as well as minerals like iron, magnesium, and selenium. They also have a lot of good nutrients that help to ensure that you stay healthy, even though you are going on a fast.

Other foods that are not on this list should be limited, but just because you are on a fast, it doesn't mean that you can't enjoy an occasional treat. Eating a snack after supper is not going to make much of a difference in the grand scheme of things, as long as you are careful to only indulge on occasion. Moderation is key when you work with this kind of fast.

As you can see, the rules for what you are allowed to eat when you are doing an intermittent fast are simple to work with. It's mostly a matter of making sure that you eat at the right time and that you stick to a decent calorie goal. When all of these are combined properly, you will start to see the weight loss and feel healthier

Chapter 4: Fasting vs. Non-Fasting Days

Now that you know a little bit about the foods that you can have while fasting, it's important to know how the different days during the fast work. This will make it easier for you to learn the rules of intermittent fasting so that you know what to expect when you are doing the fast.

The first thing to understand about this diet is the difference between fasting days and non-fasting days. Let's take a look at the fasting days first. The 5:2 fast allows you to eat during the fasting days but asks you to restrict your calories, you will need to limit your intake to 500 calories a day if you are a woman and 600 calories a day if you are a man; this is just enough to ensure that you get some good nutrition in, but not enough to stop your body from burning fat.

During fasting days, you can use your daily calorie allowance in whatever way you choose to spend it. For instance, some people choose to just go with one big meal because it helps them to splurge a bit when they are eating. When they're done, they don't have to fret over what they are going to eat for the rest of the day. Others like to split those calories up into a few meals because it helps them to better manage their hunger. You can go with whatever method you would like as long as you are able to stay within the calorie allotment that you are given.

When choosing your meals, make sure that you are going with healthier options. You can pick a big piece of cake to cover your 500 calories if you'd like, but you probably won't feel full or satisfied afterwards. When you feel hungry, a short time later you will likely regret your decision to indulge. Making wise decisions while fasting puts yourself in a better position to manage your hunger.

You should choose one or two days during the week to fast; you will not want to do more than this during the week. In addition, make sure that you split the days up so that you do not have two fasting days back to back; this is key to preventing your body from panicking from a lack of food, putting you into starvation mode. The best way to choose when to fast is to pick two days during your week when you expect to be pretty busy and use those as your fasting days. When you keep busy with work, it will help keep your mind off food and hunger.

Moving on to the non-fasting days, these are going to be your regular days, when you will not have to fast or worry about your calories as much. However, you should still eat healthily and not to go crazy with the number of calories that you consume when you're on your non-fasting days. Otherwise, you will minimize the benefits that you are getting from those fasting days.

Ultimately, you want to make sure that you are eating normally on the non-fasting days. Your focus should be on eating healthy foods such as vegetables, fruits, whole grains, nuts, seeds, and lean, white meats, since these will provide you with the essential minerals and nutrients. However, outside of your fasting days, you will not need to worry about counting the calories as much.

Chapter 5: Fasting Day Recipes

Blueberry Compote and Yogurt

This is a great recipe that you are going to want to make all the time on your fasting days. It only takes a few minutes to make and is perfect for when you're trying to get out of the door in the morning.

What's in it

- Bran (1 tsp.)
- Fat-free yogurt (3 Tbsp.)
- Blueberries (50 pcs.)

How's it done

1. Take out a bowl and place the blueberries inside. Place the bowl in the microwave and heat on a high setting for about 45 seconds so that the blueberries will start to burst.
2. Take the bowl out of the microwave and let it cool down a bit.
3. When the blueberries are cooked, top with the bran and the yogurt before serving.

Notes:

You can also choose to make this with other berries and fruits (such as raspberries, blackberries, bananas, etc.) if you would like, though it may change the calorie count slightly.

Nutrition:

Calories: 75

Carbs: 11 g

Fat: 5 g

Protein: 1 g

Swiss and Pear Omelet

This is a delicious omelet that is sure to fill you up no matter what time of day it is. You can have it as a hot breakfast or save it for the end of the day as a quick snack.

What's in it

- Shredded Swiss cheese (1.5 oz.)
- Almond milk (1.5 Tbsp.)
- Eggs (3 pcs.)
- Salt (0.25 tsp.)

- Chopped pear (0.25 pc.)
- Diced shallot (1 pc.)
- Olive oil (1 Tbsp.)

How's it done

1. Heat up a skillet. While it's heating up, chop up a pear into thin slices. When the skillet is warm, add the salt, chopped pear, and shallot and cook for 5 minutes.
2. While that is cooking, take out a bowl and whisk together the almond milk and eggs. Pour this on top of the chopped pear to cook.
3. Once you see that the edges are turning white and the bottom has started to cook, flip your omelet over.
4. Add the cheese to the middle and fold the omelet in half. Cook a bit longer to melt the cheese.

Notes:

This omelet tastes great with other fruits as well if you would like to mix it up.

Nutrition:

Calories: 121

Carbs: 8 g

Fat: 12 g

Protein: 14 g

Breakfast Quesadillas

These quesadillas are simple and can be completed in a few minutes, making them perfect for all of your fasting days.

What's in it

- Chopped green onion (1 pc.)
- Egg (1 pc.)
- Tortilla (1 pc.)
- Salt
- Chili powder
- Water (0.5 Tbsp.)

- Chunky salsa (0.5 Tbsp.)
- Refried beans (0.5 Tbsp.)
- Cheddar cheese (2 Tbsp.)

How's it done

1. Start by whisking the water and the egg together with the chili powder.
2. Place a skillet over the stove and heat it up. Cook the green onion until it is tender and then reduce the heat to a medium setting.
3. Pour your egg mixture into this and then stir around until it is the desired consistency. Turn the heat off and cover this up to keep it warm.
4. On a clean counter, spread the tortilla out and add the salsa and beans. Add the egg on top of this and then top it all with cheese.
5. Wipe the skillet clean and place on a low flame. Heat this through, then add the quesadilla, and cook for a few minutes on each side.
6. Move the dish to a plate and then keep it warm before serving.

Notes:

Make a few servings of this at a time and then freeze the leftovers to use later on. This can make meal preparation even easier.

Nutrition:

Calories: 190

Carbs: 25 g

Fat: 11 g

Protein: 8 g

Ham and Asparagus Casserole

Nothing tastes better than a nice casserole in the morning. This one makes four servings so you can choose to eat it with your family or save it for later.

What's in it

- Cheddar cheese (0.5 c.)
- Cooked ham (0.5 c.)
- Flour (0.5 c.)
- Nonfat milk (1 c.)
- Chopped asparagus (2 pcs.)
- Eggs (4 pcs.)

- Chopped red bell pepper (1 pc.)
- Chopped onion (1 pc.)
- Pepper
- Salt
- Tarragon (0.25 tsp.)
- Parmesan (2 Tbsp.)

How's it done

1. Allow the oven to heat up to 425 degrees. Grease up a baking dish with cooking spray. Spread out the ham on the bottom and then follow with the bell pepper, onion, and asparagus.
2. Take out a bowl and whisk together the salt, pepper, dried tarragon, milk, flour, Parmesan cheese, and eggs.
3. When the egg mixture is mixed, pour it over the other ingredients inside your baking dish. Add the baking dish to the oven and let it bake.
4. After 10 minutes, the casserole should be set and you can take it out of the oven. Add the cheddar cheese and then bake two more minutes so the cheese can melt.

5. Allow it to stand on the cooling rack for a few minutes before serving.

Notes:

This casserole tastes great either warm or cold, so consider taking it to work on your fasting days.

Nutrition:

Calories: 190

Carbs: 5 g

Fat: 11 g

Protein: 12 g

Italian Chicken

There is nothing easier than throwing a nice chicken dinner together. The chicken will provide you with enough protein to keep you full on your fasting days.

What's in it

- Cooking spray
- Salt

- Pepper
- Italian seasoning (0.5 tsp.)
- Balsamic vinegar(1 Tbsp.)
- Feta cheese (2 Tbsp.)
- Sliced Roma tomato (1 pc.)
- Chicken breasts (2 pcs.)

How's it done

1. Turn on the oven to a broil setting. Take out your broiler pan and spray it with some cooking spray.
2. Rinse the chicken off and then blot dry with some paper towels. Season the chicken with the pepper, salt, and Italian seasoning.
3. Lay the chicken onto your prepared broiler pan and then broil for 5 minutes on each side until the chicken reaches 165 degrees.
4. Place two tomato slices on each chicken breast and add the cheese to the top. Spoon the balsamic vinegar over it all.
5. Place this back into the oven and let it broil for another 3 minutes until the cheese is pale brown. Move to a serving dish and serve.

Notes:

You can try adding a different type of cheese like Cheddar or Pepper Jac to this to give a different flavoring to the whole dish.

Nutrition:
Calories: 220

Carbs: 11 g

Fat: 12 g

Protein: 23 g

Potato and Beef Soup

Nothing tastes better and fills you up more than some nice, hot soup on a cold day. Add this dish to your meal plan for fasting days. Feel free to make a large batch and store portions in the freezer for an easy meal later.

What's in it

- Cooking spray
- Cumin (0.5 tsp.)
- Chopped cilantro (2 tbsp.)
- Red or Yukon Gold potatoes (1.5 c.)
- Water (1.5 c.)

- Diced tomatoes (2 c.)
- Diced onion (1 pc.)
- Beef sirloin steak (0.5 lb.)

How's it done

1. Rinse off the beef steak and blot it dry. Slice into smaller cubes and set aside.
2. Coat the inside of a heavy stew pot with some cooking spray and then set it on the stove to get hot.
3. Add in the prepared beef to the stew pot and cook until the pieces are browned all over which will take about five minutes. Stir in the onion and let it cook until it is tender.
4. Stir in the water, cumin, and tomatoes. Mix this well and bring it to a boil. When this is boiling, reduce the temperatore to medium and then cover and simmer for about 20 minutes.
5. Uncover the pot and then stir in the cubed potatoes. Cover this and let it simmer for a bit longer until both the beef and the potatoes are tender, which will take another 10 minutes.

6. At this time, turn the heat off and let it stand, with the cover on, for about 5 minutes.
7. Ladle this into some soup bowls and then serve.

Notes:

Double this recipe and then freeze it to use on another day when you are busy. You can also add some more vegetables, like peas and carrots to make this a healthier option to go with for just a few more calories.

Nutrition:

Calories: 200
Carbs: 10 g
Fat: 11 g
Protein: 12 g

Lemon Flounder

Consider adding more fish to your diet even on your fasting days. This one is going to be so satisfying and will help you get all the nutrition that you need to keep you healthy and happy.

What's in it

- Snow peas, chopped (0.25 c.)

- Baby corn (0.25 c.)
- Diced carrots (0.25 c.)
- Baby peas (0.25 c.)
- Chicken broth (0.75 c.)
- Red onion, sliced (0.5)
- Halved flounder fillet (0.5 lb.)
- Drill, dried (0.25 tsp.)
- Lemon pepper seasoning (1 tsp.)
- Cornstarch (1 Tbsp.)

How's it done

1. To get started with this recipe, take out a pan and heat it up to a high heat on the stove. Pour on the chicken broth before adding the lemon pepper seasoning, dill, and sliced onion.
2. Cover and let this simmer for another 3 minutes until the onion is tender.
3. Uncover the pan and then stir in the snow peas, corn, diced carrots, and baby peas. Add the flounder to the top of the ingredients and simmer for another 5 minutes so that the fish can cook all the way through.

4. Move the fish to a bowl using a slotted spoon and then cover to keep the fish warm.
5. Take a bit of the broth out of the soup and add to the bowl. Stir in the cornstarch before adding this back to the pan. Stir it well and bring to a boil.
6. Pour the broth and vegetables on top of the fish and then serve.

Notes:

You can add a nice side salad with some homemade dressing if you still need to get a few calories to get to your 500 or 600 calories for the day.

Nutrition:

Calories: 190

Carbs: 2 g

Fat: 10 g

Protein: 14 g

Pork Carnitas

These pork carnitas are quick and easy to make. You can always save yourself time by making extra pork and freezing it - you'll thank yourself later when you feel tired from a busy day and the only thing you'll have to do is reheat your leftovers.

What's in it

- Pepper
- Salt (0.25 tsp.)
- Dark molasses (0.5 Tbsp.)
- Orange juice (0.5 Tbsp.)
- Brown sugar (1 Tbsp.)
- Minced garlic clove (1 pc.)
- Pork tenderloin (0.5 lb.)

How's it done

1. Rinse off the pork tenderloin and blot it down with some paper towels. Slice thinly and then set it aside.
2. Place a skillet on a flame and then heat it through. Once it is hot, add the pork tenderloin. Cook these for about 4 minutes until the pork is tender and cook it through.
3. Drain out the oil before stirring in the pepper, salt, molasses, orange juice, and brown sugar.
4. Stir this around and simmer until your sauce is thick. Turn off the heat and let it stand for a few minutes to thicken before serving.

Notes:

You can add a little bit more garlic to the mix if you feel that you need some more flavor to the meal. Add the pork to a few tortillas or to some lettuce leaves to complete the meal.

Nutrition:

Calories: 180

Carbs:: 2 g

Fat: 9 g

Protein: 14 g

Chapter 6: Nonfasting Day Breakfasts

Mini Quiche's

Quiches are easy to make, and they are perfect if you're on the go. Perfect for breakfast or a mid-day snack, these quiches have all the protein you need to stay satisfied all day long.

What's in it

- Olive oil (2 tsp.)

- Pepper (0.25 tsp.)
- Salt (0.5 tsp.)
- Rosemary (1 Tbsp.)
- Parmesan cheese (0.75 c.)
- Egg whites (6 pcs.)
- Eggs (5 pcs.)
- Cooking spray
- Baby spinach (3 oz.)
- Mushrooms (6 oz.)
- Minced garlic cloves (1 pc.)
- Chopped red onion (0.5 pc.)

How's it done

1. Turn on the oven and allow it to heat up to 350 degrees. Coat some muffin tins with cooking spray and add some liners into each one.
2. In a bowl, whisk together the pepper, salt, rosemary, Parmesan cheese, egg whites, and eggs to make them fluffy.
3. Take out a skillet and heat up the olive oil inside. Add the garlic and onion until they are fragrant. Now add in the mushrooms and then cook for another 5 minutes.

4. Take the pan off the heat and let it cool down a little bit. Place some of this mixture into each of the prepared muffin cups and add some spinach on the top.

5. Slowly pour the egg mixture into each cup and fill to the rim. Add these to the oven and let them bake.

6. After 25 minutes, take them out of the oven and allow them to cool down before serving.

Notes:

You will find that by using some paper muffin liners to make the quiche, you can save time on clean up.

Nutrition (1 mini quiche):

Calories: 83
Carbs: 2 g
Fat: 5 g
Protein: 8 g

Sweet Potato Pancakes

These pancakes pack 18 grams of protein in each serving and offer plenty of vitamins to keep you healthy and strong. This quick and easy meal is a fantastic, balanced breakfast to start your day off great.

What's in it

- Maple syrup (1.5 Tbsp.)
- Nutmeg (0.25 tsp.)
- Cinnamon (1 tsp.)
- Egg whites (4 pcs.)
- Eggs (5 pcs.)
- Oats (1.5 c.)
- Cottage cheese (1.5 c.)
- Sweet potatoes (2 pcs.)

How's it done

1. Allow the oven some time to heat up to 400 degrees. Take your potatoes and prick them a few times with a fork. Add them to a baking sheet and let them cook for a bit.

2. After 50 minutes, take the potatoes out of the oven and carefully slit them lengthwise. Allow these to cool a bit before scooping the flesh of the potatoes into the blender.

3. Add the syrup, nutmeg, cinnamon, egg whites, eggs, oats, and cottage cheese into the blender. Blend this until it is smooth.

4. Now, take out a big skillet and prepare it with some cooking spray. When this is hot, after two

minutes, scoop some of the batter onto the skillet and cook so that the pancakes become golden brown, which will take about 4 minutes on each side.

5. Repeat with the rest of the batter and then serve warm.

Notes:

You can make this recipe a few times and then store in the freezer for up to 3 months. This makes it easier for you to just defrost them the night before and have them ready for those busy days.

Nutrition:

Calories: 238

Carbs: 28 g

Fat: 6 g

Protein: 18 g

Cherry and Almond Breakfast Cookies

Who would have thought that cookies can make a healthy breakfast? These small cookies are full of fruit, nuts, and whole grains which provide an excellent source of nutrition in the morning. These are also great to take with you and eat on the go.

What's in it

- Baking soda (1 tsp.)
- Whole-wheat flour (2.25 c.)
- Rolled oats (0.5 c.)
- Cooking spray

- Sliced raw almonds (1 c.)
- Chopped tart cherries, dried (1 c.)
- Vanilla (1 tsp.)
- Eggs (2 pcs.)
- Maple syrup (0.5 c.)
- Brown sugar (0.5 c.)
- Plain Greek yogurt (0.5 c.)
- Applesauce (0.5 c.)
- Salt (0.25 tsp.)

How's it done

1. Allow the oven to heat up to 350 degrees. Take a few baking sheets and line with some parchment paper.
2. Take out a bowl and combine the salt, baking soda, flour, and oats.
3. In a second bowl, whisk together the Greek yogurt and applesauce. When those are mixed, add the maple syrup and brown sugar until the mixture is smooth. Add the vanilla and the eggs and mix to smooth the mixture together.
4. Slowly fold the dry ingredients into the wet ones and stir to combine. Now, add the

almonds and cherries, making sure that they are well distributed in the batter.

5. Add 2 tablespoons of batter onto a baking sheet to make each cookie and then flatten them down a little bit. Place in the oven to bake.

6. After 15 minutes, you can take the cookies out and let them cool before serving or storing.

Notes:

You will find that these tart cherries are a great source of a lot of nutrients that the body needs. Eating a few of these each day will help you to get going and feel great, even while cheating a little bit.

Nutrition:

Calories: 214
Carbs: 36 g
Fat: 6 g
Protein: 6 g

Apple Walnut Loaf

This is going to remind you of all the delicious food that you enjoyed at grandma's house when you were younger. Made with healthy ingredients, you can enjoy this tasty treat without worrying that you might consume too many calories.

What's in it

- Applesauce (0.5 c.)
- Cinnamon (0.5 tsp.)
- Salt (0.5 tsp.)
- Baking soda (1 tsp.)
- All-purpose flour (1 c.)

- Whole-wheat flour (1 c.)
- Cooking spray
- Chopped walnuts (0.5 c.)
- Chopped Rome apple (1 pc.)
- Unsweetened almond milk (0.5 c.)
- Egg (1 pc.)
- Honey (0.5 c.)

How's it done

1. Allow the oven to heat up to 325 degrees. Prepare a loaf pan with some cooking spray.
2. Take out a medium bowl and sift together the all-purpose and whole-wheat flours with the cinnamon, salt, and baking soda.
3. In another bowl, combine the honey and applesauce and stir it together until it is combined. Add the almond milk and egg and stir well.
4. Fold the dry ingredients into this, but be careful about overmixing. Fold in the walnuts and the apples in as well, making sure to distribute them throughout the batter.

5. Pour this batter into a loaf pan and spread it out evenly. Add this to the oven and allow to bake for almost an hour.

6. After 55 minutes, you can take the pan out of the oven and cool for 5 minutes and slice it up.

Notes:

You can keep this in a plastic container at room temperature for up to 5 days or freeze for a few days as well to eat later.

Nutrition:

Calories: 206
Carbs: 45 g
Fat: 2 g
Protein: 5 g

Blueberry Scones

It is hard to give up those sweet treats when you are on a diet. With these scones, you'll have the perfect excuse to satisfy your sweet tooth without feeling guilty. These scones are packed full of nutritious ingredients like Greek yogurt, whole-grains, and blueberries.

What's in it

- Salt (0.5 tsp.)
- Baking powder (4 tsp.)
- Whole-wheat flour (0.75 c.)
- Flour (1.25 c.)

- Cooking spray
- Wild blueberries (1 c.)
- Vanilla (1 tsp.)
- Milk (0.5 c.)
- Greek yogurt (1 c.)
- Canola oil (3 Tbsp.)
- Egg (1 pc.)
- Sugar (0.5 c.)
- Baking soda (0.25)

How's it done

1. Allow the oven to heat up to 400 degrees. Take out two baking sheets and cover with cooking spray.
2. In a bowl, sift together both the flours with the baking soda, salt, and baking powder.
3. In a second bowl, add the vanilla, milk, yogurt, oil, egg, and sugar. Fold the dry ingredients in with the wet ingredients until they are combined.
4. Fold in the blueberries and the drop some of the batter onto the baking sheets. Place the baking pans into the oven.

5. After 15 minutes, take the scones out of the oven and let them cool down before serving.

Notes:

When blueberries are not in season, it is fine to go with frozen ones. The wild blueberries are good to add into the scones because they have plenty of nutrients and antioxidants that your body needs to get going in the morning.

Nutrition:

Calories: 160

Carbs: 26 g

Fat: 4 g

Protein: 5 g

Chapter 7: Nonfasting Day Lunches

Grilled Steak Salad

There is nothing as satisfying to eat for lunch than this salad. With fresh greens to provide you with the right vitamins, minerals, and healthy protein to keep you strong, you'll be sure to enjoy this favorite again and again.

What's in it

- Cucumber, sliced (1 pc.)
- Halved cherry tomatoes (1 c.)
- Mixed greens (1 package)
- Flank steak (1 lb.)
- Soy sesame dressing
- Grated carrot (1 pc.)

How's it done

1. Take out a bowl and add in the steak with some of the dressing. Make sure that all your steak is covered with the dressing and then set aside for a minimum of 30 minutes to marinate.
2. After the steak has had some time to marinate, turn on the grill, and get it preheated. Place the steak on the grill and get rid of the extra marinade.
3. Let the steak grill until it reaches 145 degrees, which will take about 5 minutes on each side.

Move the steak to a plate and allow the steak to rest for a bit before slicing.

4. Place some of the greens on four different plates and top with the carrots, cucumbers, and tomatoes. Layer the steak across the bowl. Drizzle with some of the dressing and then serve.

Notes:

You can make your own mixed greens if you like. You can add in any combination of greens, such as arugula, butter lettuce, red lead lettuce, radicchio, and spinach.

Nutrition:

Calories: 433
Carbs: 10 g
Fat: 35 g
Protein: 24 g

Turkey Walnut Salad

If you have any extra turkey leftover from another meal, especially around the holidays, this is a fantastic recipe for you to try. It's easy to put together and will help you feel satisfied when fasting.

What's in it

- Chopped walnuts (0.25 c.)
- Chopped celery (1 pc.)
- Chopped yellow onion (0.5 pc.)
- Minced turkey (8 oz.)

- Pepper
- Salt
- Parsley (2 tsp.)
- Lemon juice (1 tsp.)
- Dijon mustard (1 Tbsp.)
- Greek yogurt (2 Tbsp.)
- Mayo (2 Tbsp.)
- Dried cranberries (3 Tbsp.)

How's it done

1. Take out a bowl and combine the cranberries, walnuts, celery, onion, and turkey.
2. In another bowl, combine the pepper, salt, parsley, lemon juice, mustard, Greek yogurt, and mayo.
3. Top this second bowl on top of the turkey mixture and stir it well before serving.

Notes:

If you are worried about how much mayo is inside the bowl, and the extra calories it contains, you can substitute with some Greek yogurt.

Nutrition:

Calories: 175
Carbs: 8 g
Fat: 8 g
Protein: 17 g

Turkey Burgers

Turkey Burgers hit all the right notes for a traditionally satisfying meal. High in protein, quick, and easy, this is sure to be a favorite for lunch or dinner. The feta and the spinach help bind the burgers together and will add a little more flavor to the dish. Enjoy with some yogurt as a sauce to give your burger a whole new layer of taste.

What's in it

- Cooking spray
- Pepper (0.25 tsp.
- Dried oregano (1 tsp.)

- Minced garlic clove (1 pc.)
- Feta (0.25 c.)
- Chopped red onion (0.25)
- Spinach (6 oz.)
- Ground turkey (1 lb.)
- *Yogurt sauce*
- Minced garlic clove (0.5)
- Salt (0.25 tsp.)
- Dill (1 Tbsp.)
- Lemon juice (2 Tbsp.)
- Greek yogurt (1 c.)

How's it done

1. Start by making the burger patties. Take out a bowl and combine the pepper, oregano, garlic, feta, onion, spinach, and turkey.
2. Use your hands to form this mixture into four patties.
3. Add some cooking spray to the grill and then add the burger patties onto it. Cook these on a high temperature until they reach 165 degrees which takes about five minutes on each side.

4. When the burgers are done, take them off the grill and set aside to cool.
5. Now, it's time to make the yogurt sauce. Take out a bowl and combine the salt, dill, lemon juice, Greek yogurt, and garlic. Stir the ingredients until they are combined.
6. When you are ready to serve, top some of this yogurt sauce on top of each burger.

Notes:

You can choose to place your burger on a whole grain bun with some of your favorite toppings such as tomato and lettuce.

Nutrition:

Calories: 248
Carbs: 6 g
Fat: 12 g
Protein: 30 g

Thai Chicken Stir Fry

Stir-fries are one of the best things that you can make when you need to feed the whole family that is fresh, easy, and quick. They also allow you to introduce some different flavors to the meal to keep things new and interesting.

What's in it

- Brown rice (1 c.)
- Water (3 c.)
- Thai marinade (0.33 c.)

- Chicken breast, sliced (1.25 lbs.)
- Sliced red bell pepper (1 pc.)
- Sliced white mushrooms (8 oz.)
- Sliced broccoli (0.5 head)
- Canola oil (1 Tbsp.)

How's it done

1. Take out a big bowl and add the chicken strips with your marinade. Toss around to coat, then cover the bowl, and let it marinate for at least 30 minutes or overnight.
2. Now, boil some water in a medium pot. Add the brown rice and lower the heat a little bit to medium. Cover and let the rice simmer for 40 minutes so that it becomes tender.
3. After about 40 minutes, drain out the extra water and then move the rice over to a bowl to let it cool.
4. Take out a skillet and heat up the oil until it starts to shimmer. Add the chicken, without the leftover marinade, and cook so that it browns on all sides.

5. Now, add the bell pepper, mushrooms, and broccoli. Let these cook until they start to soften, which will take about 8 minutes.
6. Add some of the reserved marinade and cook another minute before serving.

Notes:

If you have a rice cooker, you can choose to use that to cook your rice. This recipe also works to help with some other grains as well, such as quinoa and farro.

Nutrition:

Calories: 357

Carbs: 46 g

Fat: 3 g

Protein: 24 g

Beef Mushroom Meatballs

These mushroom meatballs are perfect for your fasting days. Their compact size means they can be eaten as a snack, added to a salad, or served as the main dish.

What's in it

- Minced garlic cloves (2 pc.)
- Parsley, chopped (0.5 c.)
- Breadcrumbs (0.75 c.)
- Ground beef (1 lb.)
- Chopped Portobello mushrooms (1 container)

- Safflower oil (1 Tbsp.)
- Pepper (0.25 tsp.)
- Salt (0.25 tsp.)
- Beaten egg (1 pc.)

How's it done

1. To start this recipe, take a skillet out and heat up some oil until it is shimmering. Add the chopped mushrooms, cook them for 5 minutes to soften them up, and then remove the mushrooms from the heat so they can cool down.

2. Turn on the oven and allow it to heat up to 350 degrees. Take out a bowl and combine the pepper, salt, egg, garlic, parsley, breadcrumbs, beef, and mushrooms. Mix these together with your hands.

3. Form this mixture into balls and then place into muffin cups. Place in the oven and let them bake.

4. After 25 minutes, take the meatballs out of the oven and let them cool before serving or storing.

Notes:

When you are ready to mix the ground beef together with the mushrooms, you will find that a ratio of 1 to 1 is the best to get good flavor.

Nutrition:

Calories: 232
Carbs: 12 g
Fat: 12 g
Protein: 19 g

Chapter 8: Nonfasting Day Dinners

Beef and Lentil Meatloaf

Ground beef blends go well with legumes and vegetable to make this a healthy yummy dish. Besides, who doesn't love having a meatloaf for supper!?

What's in it

- Lentils (1 can)
- Minced garlic clove (1 pc.)
- Chopped onion (0.5 pc.)
- Chopped mushrooms (1 container)
- Ground beef (1 lb.)

- Tomato sauce (0.75 c.)
- Pepper (0.25 tsp.)
- Salt (0.5 tsp.)
- Panko bread crumbs (1 c.)
- Beaten egg (1 pc.)
- Cilantro (0.5 c.)

How's it done

1. Allow the oven to heat up to 350 degrees. Take out a loaf pan and spray it with some cooking spray.
2. Take out a bowl and mix the pepper, salt, panko, egg, cilantro, lentils, garlic, onions, mushrooms, and beef together.
3. Place the meat mixture into a loaf pan and get the top to be even. Pour the tomato sauce over the top. Add the pan to the oven.
4. Bake this for about an hour until the meatloaf is cooked all the way through. Let it cool down and slice into eight portions for serving.

Notes:

Panko is basically Japanese for breadcrumbs. If you have any extra bread or other bread crumbs around the house, it is fine to use those as well.

Nutrition:

Calories: 210

Carbs: 18 g

Fat: 7 g

Protein: 19 g

Stuffed Pepper

Stuffed peppers are a homemade classic that you will want to make over and over again. This version includes more whole grains, legumes, and veggies to give you more nutrients. You can add other ingredients to the stuffing to make something new for dinner every night.

What's in it

- Chickpeas (1 c.)
- Ground beef (1 lb.)
- Cooking spray

- Farro (1 c.)
- Water (3 c.)
- Bell peppers, any color (8 pcs.)
- Pepper (0.25 tsp.)
- Salt (0.5 tsp.)
- Lemon juice (1 Tbsp.)
- Olive oil (3 Tbsp.)
- Feta cheese (0.33 c.)
- Chopped yellow onion (0.5)
- Chopped parsley (1 bunch)
- Cherry tomatoes (1 c.)

How's it done

1. Take out a pot and bring two cups of water to a boil. Add the farro and let it to simmer until all the water is absorbed and your grain is tender, which takes 30 minutes.
2. After the farro is done cooking, drain off the excess liquid and allow it to cool down for a bit. Cover and let it set in the fridge for 30 minutes.
3. Turn on the oven and heat it up to 350 degrees. Prepare a baking dish with some cooking spray.

4. Take out a big bowl and combine the onion, parsley, tomatoes, chickpeas, and beef. Then add the feta cheese and the chilled farro.

5. In a small bowl, whisk together the black pepper, salt, lemon juice, and olive oil. Pour this mixture in with your beef mixture and stir to combine.

6. Take out your peppers and slice the tops off. Remove all the membranes and the seeds from the peppers and then spoon in the beef mixture.

7. Add the peppers to a baking dish, leaving a little bit of room between them. Cover this dish with some foil and then place into the oven to bake.

8. After 50 minutes, take the foil from the baking dish and let these bake for a little bit longer. After 20 more minutes, you can take them out and serve.

Notes:

You are able to store the cooled down peppers inside a dish for up to 2 months and let them thaw overnight.

You can reheat a pepper in the microwave for a few minutes and then serve.

Nutrition:

Calories: 320
Carbs: 30 g
Fat: 14 g
Protein: 19 g

Beef Stew

On cold nights, nothing tastes better than some beef stew on the stove. You can also consider adding green beans or peppers to add more flavor to the dish.

What's in it

- Beef stew meat (1.5 lb.)
- Sweet potatoes (1.25 lbs.)
- Chickpeas (1 can)
- Pepper (0.25 tsp.)
- Salt (0.25 tsp.)
- Paprika (1 tsp.)

- Dried thyme (1 tsp.)
- Worcestershire sauce (1 Tbsp.)
- Tomato paste (2 Tbsp.)
- Beef broth (2.5 c.)
- Bay leaves (3 pcs.)
- Minced garlic cloves (2 pcs.)
- Diced celery stalk (1 pc.)
- Diced yellow onion (1 pc.)
- Peas (1 c.)
- Baby carrots (1 c.)

How's it done

1. Take out your slow cooker and add the bay leaves, garlic, celery, onion, peas, carrots, sweet potatoes, chickpeas, and meat inside.
2. In a bowl, whisk together the pepper, salt, paprika, thyme, Worcestershire sauce, tomato paste, and beef broth. Pour this mixture into the slow cooker.
3. Cover up the slow cooker and then cook on a high setting for about 6 hours and serve.

Notes:

This beef stew is considered almost like a soup because it is a little thinner. If you would like to make it thicker, you can add in some of the liquid from the slow cooker with some flour and then stir back into the stew. Cook for another 30 minutes before serving.

Nutrition:

Calories: 518
Carbs: 59 g
Fat: 10 g
Protein: 49 g

Slow Cooker Brisket

Slow cooker meals are the best for those busy days. Just throw the meat in the slow cooker in the morning and come home to a delicious home cooked meal.

What's in it

- Lager beer (1 bottle)
- Beef brisket (3 lb.)
- Pepper (0.25 tsp.)
- Salt (0.5 tsp.)
- Cumin (0.5 tsp.)

- Smoked paprika (0.5 tsp.)
- Instant coffee crystals (1 tsp.)
- Brown sugar (1 Tbsp.)

How's it done

1. Take out a bowl and combine the pepper, salt, cumin, paprika, coffee crystals, and brown sugar.
2. Using your hands, you can rub this mixture all over the brisket. Set up the slow cooker to a high setting before adding the brisket inside.
3. Pour the beer all over the brisket and then place the lid on top of the slow cooker.
4. Cover the slow cooker and cook it on high for about 6 hours. When the brisket is done, allow it to cool for about 10 minutes. Then slice or shred up the meat before serving.

Notes:

You can serve the brisket with any kind of side that you would like. Carrots, potatoes, sweet potatoes, or other vegetables can be nice. If you have a lot of leftovers, consider serving it for a baked potato, on a salad, or for tacos.

Nutrition:

Calories: 459
Carbs: 3 g
Fat: 13 g
Protein: 74 g

Lamb Chops

Lamb is a great source of protein to help keep your muscles strong. Add some vegetables to the mix, and you are sure to have a meal that you will want to try again and again.

What's in it

- Pepper (0.25 tsp.)
- Salt (0.25 tsp.)
- Dry white wine (2 Tbsp.)
- Greek yogurt (1 c.)

- Minced garlic cloves (4 pcs.)
- Mint leaves (0.75 c.)
- Lamb chops (8 pcs.)
- Cooking spray

How's it done

1. In a bowl, mix together some pepper, salt, all of the wine, half a cup of yogurt, three garlic cloves, and half a cup of mint.
2. Add the lamb to this and toss around to coat. Place this bowl in the fridge to marinate for about an hour.
3. Turn on your grill or prepare a grill pan with some cooking spray and place it over medium-high heat.
4. While your lamb is marinating, you can make the yogurt sauce. In a bowl, whisk together the pepper, salt, and the rest of the yogurt, garlic, and mint.
5. Take the lamb out of the marinade and place it onto the grill. Cook for about 12 minutes until the inside of the lamb reaches around 145 degrees.

6. When you are ready to serve, place two chops on a plate and have 2 tablespoons of yogurt sauce on the side to enjoy later.

Notes:

You can store any of the leftovers for about a week. This can make it an easy lunch when you are too busy to make something.

Nutrition:

Calories: 300
Carbs: 3 g
Fat: 4 g
Protein: 46 g

Chapter 9: Healthy Snacks to Help You Out

Peanut Butter Energy Cookies

For those times you find yourself craving something sweet, these cookies make the perfect healthy snack. These tasty treats are a healthy way to curb cravings while giving you a much-needed boost of energy.

What's in it

- Peanut butter, creamy (0.5 c.)
- Salt (0.25 tsp.)
- Baking soda (1 tsp.)
- Cocoa powder (0.25 c.)
- Flour (1 c.)
- Chopped peanuts (0.5 c.)
- Rolled oats (2 c.)
- Vanilla (1 tsp.)
- Beaten eggs (2 pcs.)
- Brown sugar (0.5 c.)
- Milk (0.5 c.)
- Greek yogurt (0.25 c.)
- Mashed banana (1 c.)

How's it done

1. Take out a bowl and sift together the salt, baking soda, cocoa powder, and flour.
2. In another bowl, stir together the milk, Greek yogurt, banana, and peanut butter. Add the

brown sugar and then stir to combine. Now, add the vanilla and the eggs and combine.

3. Add the flour to this peanut butter mixture and then the oats and peanuts and mix this with the dry ingredients until moist. Cover the bowl and place in the fridge for 30 minutes.

4. Allow the oven to heat up to 350 degrees. Take out two baking sheets and coat with some baking spray.

5. Drop some of the batter onto the baking sheets and then press them down a little bit. Place in the oven to bake.

6. After about 15 minutes, you can take the cookies out of the oven and allow them to cool down before serving.

Notes:

You can make a few batches so that you always have some cookies ready when you want to snack.

Nutrition:

Calories: 143

Carbs: 19 g

Fat: 1 g

Protein: 5 g

Orange and Apricot Bites

These bite-sized snacks are nutritious and delicious, and sure to satisfy your sweet tooth. These are also a great pick-me-up to help you through your day if you start to feel hungry.

What's in it

- Coconut (0.66 c.)
- Almond butter (0.5 c)
- Dried apricots (0.5 c.)
- Pitted dates (1.5 c.)
- Rolled oats (1 c.)
- Vanilla (1 tsp.)

- Orange juice (3 Tbsp.)
- Zest of an orange (1 Tbsp.)

How's it done

1. Allow the oven to heat up to 350 degrees. Line some parchment paper on a baking sheet. Place some oats on the baking sheet and toast them for a few minutes until they are slightly toasted.
2. While your oats are in the oven, take the food processor out and place the dates into the food processor and pulse to make smooth.
3. Add the vanilla, orange juice and zest, coconut, almond butter, apricots, and toasted oats to the food processor. Pulse so that the mixture becomes smooth. Move to a bowl.
4. Use your hands to make little balls out of the batter and place them into a resealable container. Allow these to set for at least 15 minutes and then serve.

Notes:

While the oats are gluten-free, it is important to realize that many brands will make these in a factory that may also work with gluten products. Look on the package to find out where your product is made.

Nutrition:

Calories: 117
Carbs: 17 g
Fat: 2 g
Protein: 3 g

Trail Mix

Making your own trail mix puts you in full control. You can determine what ingredients go inside so you get the best tasting trail mix. Nibble on this snack when you start to feel hungry for a nutritious boost of energy.

What's in it

- Sunflower seeds (2 Tbsp.)
- Dark chocolate chips (3 Tbsp.)
- Dried tart cherries (3 Tbsp.)
- Dried apricots (10 pcs.)
- Raw almonds (0.5 c.)

How's it done

1. To get make your trail mix, take out a bowl and add the almonds, sunflower seeds, chocolate chips, cherries, and apricots.
2. Toss all these together and then add it to a resealable container. You are able to store it in there for up to a month.

Notes:

You can easily double or triple this recipe and then split it up into smaller portions so that it is ready to go whenever you are. You can also mix up the combination of dried fruit and nuts that you are using so that you get the taste that is right for you.

Nutrition:

Calories: 216
Carbs: 18 g
Fat: 15 g
Protein: 6 g

Cinnamon Cocoa Popcorn

There is nothing better to snack on than a little bit of popcorn. Adding chocolate and cinnamon to popcorn can make this healthy snack a little bit more fun. You can mix and match a variety of toppings to get the flavor that you like best.

What's in it

- Cinnamon (1 tsp.)
- Cocoa powder (1 Tbsp.)
- Cooking spray
- Popcorn kernels (0.5 c.)
- Coconut oil (3 Tbsp.)

- Salt (1 tsp.)
- Sugar (1 Tbsp.)

How's it done

1. Take a gallon pot out and heat up the three tablespoons of coconut oil. Add three popcorn kernels, and then when one of the kernels start to pop, you know that it is hot enough. Add in the rest of the kernels.
2. Cover the pot with its lid and shake it round to make sure that there isn't any burning. When the popcorn is popped, you can add the prepared popcorn to a mixing bowl.
3. Spray your popcorn with some cooking spray. Use your hands to toss the popcorn around to mix well.
4. Sprinkle with the salt, sugar, cinnamon, and cocoa powder. Make sure that the popcorn is coated properly before serving.

Notes:

Another option is to use an air popper to pop the kernels. You can then just toss the popcorn with some melted coconut oil in a bowl before adding in the flavors.

Nutrition:

Calories: 188
Carbs: 24 g
Fat: 12 g
Protein: 3 g

Kale Chips

Kale chips are all the rage for those who are looking for a healthier alternative to traditional potato chips. Buying kale chips in stores can be expensive, and you have no control over how it's made. This recipe allows you to make kale chips from the comfort of your home and save you money in the process.

What's in it

- Salt (1 tsp.)
- Lime juice (2 Tbsp.)
- Zest of a lime (1 pc.)
- Sriracha (1 tsp.)

- Olive oil (0.25 c.)
- Cooking spray
- Torn kale (1 bag)
- Pepper (0.5 tsp.)

How's it done

1. Turn on the oven and allow it to heat up to 400 degrees. Take out two baking pans and coat them with some cooking spray.
2. In a big bowl, whisk together the black pepper, salt, lime zest and juice, sriracha, and olive oil.
3. Take out the torn kale, add it to the bowl, and then toss around until the leaves have been coated with the dressing.
4. Pour the kale into single even layers on the baking sheet. Add to the oven and let them bake.
5. After about 10 minutes, the kale should be crisp. You can take them out of the oven and allow them to cool off.

Notes:

Buying the bags of kale that are already torn up can save you a ton of time. These are usually pretty reasonably priced at most grocery stores. If you want, you can also purchase a head of kale on your own and tear it up to make these chips.

Nutrition:

Calories: 102
Carbs: 5 g
Fat: 1 g
Protein: 1 g

Chapter 10: Seven Days to a Better You

Now that you have plenty of delicious recipes to keep you company on your intermittent fasting journey, it is time to learn about some of the ways you can ensure the process is as successful as possible. You are never going to be successful with this kind of fast if you do not take some time to plan things out. Never forget, when it comes to intermittent fasting, failing to plan is the same as planning to fail.

The good news is that with a little bit of planning, the entire process becomes far easier to manage and you will be able to deal with the challenges that come with going on a fast. Here we are going to provide you with a simple meal plan that you can follow when you are on the 5:2 fast. This will show you how to split up the days, but you can split them up, however, you would like. However, you end up splitting up your fasts, just make sure that you follow a plan that you can stick with regularly for the best results. What follows is a meal plan that you can follow when you are just getting started with intermittent fasting.

Day 1: Nonfasting Day

Breakfast: Mini Quiche's

Lunch: Grilled Steak Salad

Dinner: Beef and Lentil Meatloaf

Snack: Peanut Butter Energy Cookies

Nutrition for the day

Calories: 1200

Carbs: 49 g

Fat: 48 g

Protein: 56 g

Day 2: Fasting Day

Breakfast: Blueberry Compote and Yogurt

Lunch: Italian Chicken

Dinner: Lemony Flounder

Nutrition for the day

Calories: 485

Carbs: 24 g

Fat: 26 g

Protein: 38 g

Day 3: Nonfasting Day

Breakfast: Sweet Potato Pancakes
Lunch: Turkey Walnut Salad
Dinner: Stuffed Peppers
Snack: Orange and Apricot Bites

Nutrition for the day

Calories: 1100
Carbs: 83 g
Fat: 30 g
Protein: 57 g

Day 4: Nonfasting Day
Breakfast: Cherry and Almond Breakfast Cookies
Lunch: Turkey Burgers
Dinner: Beef Stew
Snack: Trail Mix

Nutrition for the day
Calories: 1196
Carbs: 119 g

Fat: 43 g

Protein: 91 g

Day 5: Fasting Day

Breakfast: Swiss and Pear Omelet

Lunch: Potato and Beef Soup

Dinner: Pork Carnitas

Nutrition for the day

Calories: 501

Carbs: 20 g

Fat: 32 g

Protein: 40 g

Day 6: Nonfasting Day

Breakfast: Apple Walnut Loaf

Lunch: Thai Chicken Stir Fry

Dinner: Slow Cooker Brisket

Snack: Cinnamon Cocoa Popcorn

Nutrition for the day

Calories: 1210

Carbs: 118 g

Fat: 30 g

Protein: 106 g

Day 7: Nonfasting Day

Breakfast: Blueberry Scones

Lunch: Beef Mushroom Meatballs

Dinner: Lamb Chops

Snack: Kale Chips

Nutrition for the day

Calories: 1300

Carbs: 51 g

Fat: 21 g

Protein: 73 g

Chapter 11: FAQs

Getting started with the intermittent fast is a new experience. We have been told for years that we need to eat a certain way, that we shouldn't miss out on meals because we are going to go into starvation mode, that we have to eat at certain times and so many times per day, or that we will have trouble with our metabolism and staying healthy. But with intermittent fasting, all of this is thrown out the window so that you can actually get your body to burn fat and lose weight with less effort.

Naturally, this means that you may have some questions when you are first getting started. This chapter is going to answer some of the questions you may have before getting started on the intermittent fast.

What is intermittent fasting?

Intermittent fasting is a practice that humans have been using for thousands of years as a means of achieving a higher consciousness or communing with a higher power. Recently, more and more people have been practicing intermittent fasting due to its effectiveness for weight loss and other health benefits. Proponents of this new type of targeted intermittent fasting enjoy it because it doesn't require sticking to a limiting meal plan or require counting calories to see serious results.

The reason that intermittent fasting is so useful comes from the basic fact that the body behaves quite differently when it's in a fed state compared to when it's in a fasting state. A fed state is any period where the body is currently absorbing nutrients from foods it's actively digesting. This state begins roughly 5 minutes after you have finished a meal and generally lasts for about 5 hours depending on the foods you consume. While your body is ccupied, it's also creating insulin which means it's more difficult for it to burn fat as easily as it otherwise might.

You can choose which type of intermittent fast you would like to go with. Keep in mind that you're also able to eat zero-calorie gum, water, diet soda, and coffee during your fasting periods to help keep the hunger pains at bay.

Will fasting make me store fat or put me into starvation mode?

No, this is a common misconception that a lot of people have about intermittent fasting. Your metabolism is actually quite hearty and as long as you get into a routine with the way you eat and stick with it, your metabolism will be able to adjust accordingly. There are many good reasons to fast including fat loss, insulin reduction, and so much more.

There are a few key points that you can look at to determine whether this is a good diet plan to go with. First, you are going to burn fat when you are fasting. Second, you are going to burn food when you are eating. The fact is that you do not have to worry about starving as this takes much longer than the maximum 20 hours that you will go without food. Intermittent fasting tricks the body into thinking its starving, allowing you to experience many of the benefits to the metabolism being in this state has for the body, without any of the downsides.

With intermittent fasting, the longest you would go without eating is about 20 hours rather than 3 days, and most of the fasting occurs while you are sleeping. As such, it's practically impossible for intermittent fasting to damage your metabolism in the long-term.

Don't I need to eat every few hours to avoid hunger or blood sugar issues?

This is a common misconception. We have been led to believe that if we do not eat every 2-3 hours, we are going to get overly hungry or we will experience hypoglycemia from not eating. Unless you have an issue with diabetes that needs to be treated by a doctor, there is no reason that skipping a meal or two, or even fasting will result in this.

The reason that you feel hungry every few hours is that you have trained your body to be hungry frequently. The steady stream of carbs makes life easy on the body because it never has to go through and use its reserves to keep you energized. However, this often results in you gaining weight and holding onto the fat around your body. Fasting has a suppressive effect on your hunger and you will be able to eat larger portions when you break your fast which helps to satisfy your appetite. You may run into some issues of hunger during the first few days, but once you get past that, you will be fine.

What if I get hungry?

You will probably feel hungry when you first get started with intermittent fasting. This is because the body is used to having a steady stream of carbs to use for fuel and you have suddenly forced it to change its pattern. Your job during the fast, however, it to make it through until you are allowed to eat again. After a few days, you will be able to go on these fasts without feeling as hungry, and it won't take long until you are able to see the results.

Now, if you are on one of these fasts and you find that you are really hungry and want to break that fast, there are a few things that you should keep in mind:

- *Drink more water*: Sometimes, it's not hunger that is going to ruin your plans but thirst. Consider drinking a few glasses of water and see how you feel.

- *Simmer down*: It's only a short period of time until you can eat again. Think of how accomplished you will feel when you are done and how much better you will feel as a result.

- *Stay busy*: Sometimes, you are just hungry because you are sitting around and not doing anything. If you are having cravings or feel hungry, it's time to get up and move. Go to work, read a book, go for a walk, or do something that will keep you busy.

- *Discipline*: Fasting is no harder to do than some of the other diet plans that you may try. Try to stay consistent for at least a month before you make any other decisions as a result.

Are there any disadvantages to intermittent fasting?

There are many great benefits to fasting! You will be able to get your blood sugars in line, feel more energized, and have more time because you are not meal planning all the time. However, there are also a few side effects that you will need to pay attention to. For example, some people complain that they deal with nausea and headaches when they first get started with an intermittent fast. These will usually go away after a few days and can be helped by drinking more water. You may also need to go to the bathroom more often because most people increase their fluid intake when they are on a fast.

Can I stay on intermittent fasting long term?

Yes, this is a plan that you can stay on long term. And, once you get the hang of how fasting works, you are going to naturally want to stick with it because it's so easy. Intermittent fasting is not so much a diet as it is a plan for when you are able to eat and when you shouldn't. It will help you to burn fat and lose weight with less work.

Which fast should I go with?

You can choose the fast that works best for you and your lifestyle; each of can be efficient and will help you lose weight in no time. What it ultimately boils down to is personal preference and what works best for your schedule. Ideally, you will be able to find a type of intermittent fasting that works with your existing schedule because having to adapt your life around the idea of fasting just means adding another layer of difficultly to forming a new habit in the first place.

What happens if I have trouble staying on this fast?

Beginning a new lifestyle change can take some time, but the number one thing that you can do is make sure that you stick with it. Trying the intermittent fast for one day and assuming it doesn't work because you do not see immediate results is one of the worst things that you can do. Keep in mind that it takes a full 30 days to build a new habit, which means you need to stick with it for at least a month before you can hope to see your results with any degree of accuracy.

With that said, if you are having a hard time getting the intermittent fasting habit to stick, finding someone who can hold you accountable is a great way to get started and stat consistent. See if you are able to find an online community of people who would like to work with you to hold you accountable, if not, even having a friend that you report to might be enough to get the habit to stick. While you certainly don't need other people around to ensure you lose weight, they can make it much easier to stay on course.

Conclusion

Thanks for making it through to the end of this book. Hopefully, you found it an enjoyable way to learn about intermittent fasting and meeting your weight loss goals once and for all.

The next step is to take some time to get on an intermittent fast. There is so much that you can learn about this fasting method, and it's a great way for you to easily lose weight while still eating most of the things you love in moderation. Whether you have tried weight loss plans in the past or are just getting started, this guidebook will help you get started with intermittent fasting. If the information provided in the previous chapters work for you, there is no reason you shouldn't be able to find the results you are looking for thanks to intermittent fasting.

Review Request

If you enjoyed this book or found it useful, then I'd like to ask you for a quick favor: would you be kind enough to leave a review for this book on Amazon? It'd be greatly appreciated.

Your feedback does matter and helps me to make improvements so I can provide the best content possible. Thank you!

You can leave a review here:
http://bit.ly/ultimatefastingdietreview

Thank you for your support!

Related Books

The Art of Intermittent Fasting: How to lose weight, shed fat, and live a healthier life

If you are interested in learning more, and shedding those extra pounds once and for all, then ***The Art of Intermittent Fasting*** is the book you have been waiting for...

Inside, you will learn how to use your body's natural rhythms so you can start seeing significant gains in as little as one month.

Here are just a few things covered:

- How Our Modern Diet is Failing Us
- What is intermittent fasting?
- How Can I Fast?
- The benefits of intermittent fasting
- The different types of fasts that you can go on
- The foods that you should eat on this diet plan

- How to get started with fasting
- How to exercise while fasting
- Tips for getting the most out of your workouts
- Using the ketogenic diet with intermittent fasting
- Tips to help you get going
- FAQs to help answer all your fasting questions
- meal plans you can follow to help make the intermittent fast work better for you.
- *And more...*

So, what are you waiting for? Take control of your eating habits and improve the way you look and feel once and for all, buy this book today!

Get your copy here:
http://bit.ly/artoffastingbook

The Science Of Intermittent Fasting: The Complete Guide To Unlocking Your Weight Loss Potential

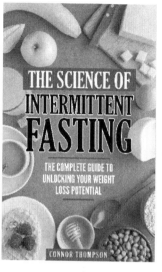

Are you thinking about losing weight or have you been trying to lose weight unsuccessfully?

Are you ready to try something that will shed those excess pounds and boost your heath?

In ***The Science of Intermittent Fasting***, you can discover how intermittent fasting could work for you, through chapters that look at:

- What intermittent fasting is all about
- Cellular repair
- Improving brain health
- Optimizing your insulin, leptin and ghrelin levels
- Inflammation
- Cholesterol
- Cancer and diabetes
- Aging
- How to get the most out of your fasts
- And lots more...

The scientific benefits of intermittent fasting on your health and weight loss are clear to see and with an in-depth look into the research and studies carried out on intermittent fasting, ***The Science of Intermittent Fasting*** is the perfect book that deliver all the answers.

Get a copy today and see for yourself how intermittent fasting can not only be good for your weight, but good for your whole body.

Get your copy now at:

http://bit.ly/thescienceoffastingbook

Made in the USA
Lexington, KY
27 September 2018